Gallery Books
Editor Peter Fallon

MARBLE

Marina Carr

MARBLE

Gallery Books

Marble
was first published
simultaneously in paperback
and in a clothbound edition
on the day of its première,
17 February 2009.

The Gallery Press
Loughcrew
Oldcastle
County Meath
Ireland

www.gallerypress.com

ISBN 978 1 85235 467 1 *paperback*
     978 1 85235 468 8 *clothbound*

A CIP catalogue record for this book
is available from the British Library.

for Dermot,
William, Daniel, Rosa, Juliette
and for Fiona Shaw
who told me a story

Characters

ART
BEN
CATHERINE
ANNE

Set

One space. One couch. One table. Two chairs. One drinks cabinet. One lamp. All use this space as if it is their own. A backdrop that can be flooded with light and indigo sky for the 'marble' passages. There should be an emptiness to the set which can take on great beauty at times. De Chirico's painting 'Melancholy and Mystery of a Street' is the mood and landscape I would like to catch: the near absence of people, the dream shadows, yet full of vibrant colour and intrigue.

Music

To underscore the 'marble' passages and to create mood during scene crossovers: possibly clarinet and strings, chant and strings. Haunting.

Time

The present.

Marble was first performed at the Abbey Theatre, Dublin, on 17 February 2009, with the following cast:

ART	Stuart McQuarrie
BEN	Peter Hanly
CATHERINE	Aisling O'Sullivan
ANNE	Derbhle Crotty

Director	Jeremy Herrin
Lighting Designer	Paul Keogan
Composer	Conor Linehan
Set and Costume Designer	Robert Innes Hopkins

ACT ONE

Scene One

ART *and* BEN *sit outside restaurant puffing on cigars and drinking brandies.*

ART And what age is she now?

BEN She'll be forty-five in December, why?

ART No reason, I dreamt about her last night.

BEN Was it a good dream?

ART It was fantastic.

BEN How so?

ART I was making love to her.

BEN Were you?

ART I never dream or I never remember them but this was so vivid. The sheets were gleaming, her legs perfect against the dazzling white.

BEN Was it in your bed or mine?

ART I've never seen your bed. It was just a bed, a room, marble somewhere, yeah marble, the floor, the windows.

BEN Marble windows?

ART Well, it was a dream.

BEN Why can't you dream about your own wife?

ART She was beside me. Why should I dream about her? Are you going fishing this weekend?

BEN I don't know. Catherine has booked tickets for the theatre.

ART What are you seeing?

BEN I forgot to ask her. She sorts all of that out. She has good taste. Generally I enjoy her choices.

ART Yeah, I read somewhere ninety per cent of theatre tickets are booked by women.

BEN Yeah, they seem to do everything. Are you planning a fishing trip?

ART I was, but the young fella's Communion is on this Saturday. But it was an amazing dream. Tell Catherine. It'll amuse her. It was so real, that's the extraordinary thing. I don't believe I've ever spoken to Catherine for more than three minutes together. But there we were as happy as — Oh God — She's a good-looking woman.

BEN She is.

ART But I've never fancied her.

BEN I would hope not.

ART Do you not like other men fancying your wife?

BEN I don't mind them looking, but any conversation on the topic I find distasteful, I suppose.

ART I love when men give Anne the once-over; feel I've made the right choice.

BEN A bit late now if you haven't, what are you, twenty years married?

ART Eighteen. We were very young. Men now are starting off at my age, older.

BEN Are you going to leave Anne?

ART Why would I do that?

BEN Well, you're dreaming about it.

ART But that's nothing. Do you mind me saying I dreamt I made love to your wife last night?

BEN I'm not sure you shouldn't have kept it to yourself.

ART You're very old-fashioned.

BEN Am I?

ART I didn't realize you were so repressed. Have you never dreamt about Anne?

BEN Would you like me to?

ART Why not? As long as it's just a dream what do I care?

BEN I never dream about sex.

ART Come off it. It was fantastic, the light was beautiful. I couldn't stop looking at her. It'll never happen again. Why do I suddenly feel guilty?

BEN Are you going to have an affair with Catherine?

ART   I can't help what I dream — I was such a powerful man in that marble room.

BEN   Were you?

ART   It was so male and female, so clear — that was the thing about it, not like when I'm awake — Does Catherine have affairs?

BEN   Not that I'm aware of.

ART   Are you telling me you're not sure?

BEN   I'm not sure about anything.

ART   But you love her?

BEN   And Anne? What do you feel about Anne?

ART   What do I feel about Anne? That's an odd question. She's one moody wagon, I'll tell you that much.

BEN   Have you told her about your dream?

ART   God, no, it would only upset her. Why should I upset her like that for no reason?

BEN   You don't mind upsetting me.

ART   Have I? Ah, forget it! I should've kept it to myself. I thought we could say anything to one another.

BEN   There is no one you can just say anything to.

ART   Is there not?

BEN   No, there's isn't.

ART   Then I've blundered.

BEN   Ah, it doesn't matter.

ART   No, I'm out of line. If you'd dreamt about Anne like that I'd probably never speak to you again.

BEN   What exactly were you doing to her?

ART   Nothing, I swear. There was a beautiful room — The door is open and I walk along this grey panelled hallway and come to this door and the light and the smell and the sound from it is intoxicating. I walk into the room holding my breath, afraid I will sully this beautiful space, that it's not for me, but someone far more deserving. And the marble glistens all around her as she lies there on the bed. I'm sorry, Ben — but just thinking about her. All of this for me? Her hair was a star-shot, splintered gold. Does Catherine dye her hair?

BEN   Yes, she does her roots. Sometimes I do them for

her. She hates hairdressers, they waste her time.

ART So her time is precious. I love that about women, they sit around doing nothing, complaining about never having a minute. But in the dream her hair was natural, a waterfall of spun gold, I was climbing all over it, I had to resist the urge to eat it.

BEN Maybe it was someone else.

ART No, it was Catherine. And her hair was golden.

BEN She's never been golden. Catherine is dark. I don't think she'd like us talking about her like this.

ART Why not?

BEN Look, we're very happy.

ART I'm not disputing that for a minute.

BEN You are. I am a good husband and father. You have no right to speak about her like that.

ART I was just telling you a dream I had.

BEN I am the one should be dreaming about Catherine.

ART But you're not. It was my dream.

BEN About my wife.

ART What's wrong, Ben?

BEN I need to go home and see her. Make sure she's still there. Will you take care of the bill?

ART Of course — I'm sorry if I —

BEN *(Exiting)* It's nothing — nothing — It's nothing.

ART *looks after him, takes last puff of cigar, exits.*

Scene Two

CATHERINE *enters in a bathrobe with a towel on her head. She drinks from a large glass of red wine. Music in the background. Enter* BEN.

BEN   They're all asleep?

CATHERINE   You say that every evening. Yeah, they were very good, no one shouting. How was dinner?

BEN   It was fine.

CATHERINE   You had a salad, then Arrabiata with artichokes, or maybe you went crazy and had Arrabiata without artichokes.

BEN   I had steak.

CATHERINE   Very adventurous.

BEN   It was good — I'm tired.

CATHERINE   Who isn't, my darling?

BEN   Show me your hair — take the towel off.

CATHERINE   (*Flings off the towel*) My hair!

> BEN *examines her hair, a close inspection of strands.*

What?

BEN   Nothing. (*Fingers her hair dreamily, lazily*) It smells lovely. It's so dark.

CATHERINE   It's always been dark.

BEN   I dreamt last night it was blonde.

CATHERINE   I've never been blonde. Would you like me blonde?

BEN   I don't think so.

CATHERINE   And what was I doing in the dream?

BEN   You were making love.

CATHERINE   To you?

BEN   Of course to me. Why would you ask a thing like that?

CATHERINE   No reason.

BEN   Did you dream last night?

CATHERINE   As a matter of fact I did.

BEN   About me?

CATHERINE   No, about Art.

BEN Art?

CATHERINE I dreamt I was making love to him. Isn't that ridiculous? I don't know when I last saw him and there he was beaming at me, so intense, on a white, white bed, marble windows, was it? Or was it a marble door? Anyway marble, lots of marble.

BEN What's so important about marble?

CATHERINE I just remember it, the gleam off it. I shouldn't have told you. I wish it was you I dreamt about.

Kisses him.

BEN I wish it, too.

CATHERINE How is Art?

BEN You know old Art, easy company. Art is the same — he's getting on.

CATHERINE We're all getting on, none of us boys and girls any-more, and yet I still don't feel ready to be a woman — What age is he now?

BEN The same age he always was — a year younger than me.

CATHERINE I thought he was younger.

BEN He's aged. He drinks too much.

CATHERINE Well. (*Drinks, finishes glass, pours*)

BEN Talks about dying a lot.

CATHERINE Only recently have I started noticing graveyards, hearses, churches. I always thought they were some kind of decoration that had nothing to do with me, but now they follow me everywhere.

BEN Graveyards follow you?

CATHERINE You know what I mean, and dead butterflies seem to be stalking me. They appear at my feet, on the doorstep, in the bathroom, under my pillow.

BEN Yes, I know what you mean.

CATHERINE I'll be walking along or making the kids' lunches and it creeps over me, you're going to die soon, all of this will be taken from you. Impossible, but there it is.

BEN Art should stop smoking cigars. He's too old for

that sort of indulgence.

CATHERINE And you?

BEN I only smoke when I'm with him. If I get cancer it'll be his fault.

CATHERINE Has he done something on you?

BEN No, why?

CATHERINE You're very grumpy about him.

BEN Art is great. He's great.

CATHERINE And how is Anne?

BEN I think they're going through a bit of a crisis.

CATHERINE Like us?

BEN Us?

CATHERINE What sort of crisis?

BEN He's dreaming about other women.

CATHERINE What's wrong with that?

BEN He's dreaming about you.

CATHERINE About me?

BEN Last night he dreamt he was making love to you in a room full of marble.

CATHERINE Last night?

BEN Yes. Last night. While you were dreaming about him he was dreaming about you. What crisis are we going through?

CATHERINE That's fantastic. I love it.

BEN You love it?

CATHERINE Adds a bit of fizz to my life.

BEN Is your life so boring?

CATHERINE I believe it is.

BEN Do I give you such a terrible time?

CATHERINE I've no one to compare you with, have I?

BEN I'd like to know what's so fantastic about dreaming you were making love to Art?

CATHERINE We snared something in our sleep, Art and I.

BEN Art and you?

CATHERINE Yes, that's all. Darling, there is always regret for the life you didn't lead.

BEN Is there?

CATHERINE I think so, yes, the life not lived is what kills. I bet Art and Anne are very happy. They always struck me as a model couple.

BEN A model couple, what does that mean?

CATHERINE Well, all those dogs on the furniture, all those dirty children — Anne doesn't give a damn, just cooks and drinks red wine. I bet she forgets to collect them from school and they all make their way home safe and sound. I'm too conscientious, and you're looking for a row and you lied to me.

BEN When did I lie to you?

CATHERINE You didn't dream about me last night.

BEN Oh that. No, that was Art. I borrowed his dream, that's all.

CATHERINE Maybe you should dream about Anne, even it all out.

BEN Anne is not my type.

CATHERINE So now you have a type?

BEN I do. I certainly do.

CATHERINE And what is your type?

BEN You are my type.

CATHERINE I'm what life threw at you.

BEN That, too.

CATHERINE Don't forget it was I who asked you to marry me.

BEN Did you?

CATHERINE You don't remember?

BEN No, I don't. Come to think of it, I don't seem to remember making any decisions at all — Ever. Things just have the habit of happening to me.

CATHERINE So if I hadn't asked you to marry me, we wouldn't be married?

BEN But you did ask me. Did I say yes?

CATHERINE I don't remember. Did you mean to say no?

BEN I organized everything. I must've said yes or meant to. I even had to buy you a slip on the way to the church, that's what I remember most about our wedding, buying you a slip in a shop because your dress was see-through.

CATHERINE You should tell Art I dreamt about him tomorrow. And tell him there was marble in the dream, lots of marble. That's all I remember, and wild pleasure.

BEN Wild pleasure?

CATHERINE It was a good dream.

BEN Maybe the pair of you should run off together.

CATHERINE In a way we have, we seem to have managed an escape of sorts, a co-ordinated escape while staying put. What colour was my hair in the dream?

BEN Blonde. A star-seared, gold-shot blonde.

CATHERINE Yes, in my dream I was blonde, too. Should I dye my hair before it's too late?

BEN Too late for what?

CATHERINE Before I go completely grey?

BEN I like your hair dark.

CATHERINE Then dark it stays — but just for a week, a month, imagine a decade of blonde license before I'm filed for the tomb. It might be interesting to do something interesting with myself for a change.

BEN I want your hair dark.

CATHERINE It's that important to you?

BEN Yes, it is. You must remain dark.

CATHERINE And if I don't?

BEN Well, that's as good as betrayal.

CATHERINE Is it?

BEN Yes, it is — What play are we going to see on Friday?

CATHERINE Why?

BEN No reason.

CATHERINE You've never asked before.

BEN I trust your judgement.

CATHERINE And now you don't?

BEN Art was asking me.

CATHERINE I forget the name of it, about the auld one dying.

BEN Auld ones dying don't interest me. Women who've stopped ovulating should die offstage. Who cares?

CATHERINE You don't have to come.

BEN Of course I'll come. I'll probably love it.

CATHERINE Someday I'll be old, if I'm lucky.

BEN (*Examining her hair*) You need to do your roots again.

CATHERINE Why can't you bear me getting old?

BEN Women aren't allowed get old. I mean of course

you're allowed but it's not mannerly. It's somehow not appropriate. Old women interfere with my sense of myself.

CATHERINE And what about old men?

BEN Ah, men don't matter. Can't stand them. It's never about men.

CATHERINE You're wrong as usual. It's all about men, always has been, we're not even allowed grow old without your disdain.

BEN Just don't turn into one of those gangs of hags who go to flower shows.

CATHERINE Those gangs of hags look happy. They've buried their men. I could do worse than end up going to flower shows.

BEN Well, at least wait till you've trampled my grave.

CATHERINE We're talking rubbish now. It's late. I'm going to bed.

Kisses him.

See you in a while.

BEN Don't dream about Art tonight.

CATHERINE But, darling, not even you can control that.

And exit CATHERINE.

Scene Three

BEN *sits there a minute, dials on his mobile. Enter* ART *with cigar and brandy.*

ART Ben.

BEN Why aren't you in bed?

ART How do you know I'm not? I'm too tired to go to bed. Are you up?

BEN Catherine's just gone up.

ART How is she?

BEN She dreamt about you last night.

ART Oh?

BEN There was loads of marble in it.

ART Was there? Wow! Was it a good dream?

BEN It was wild and her hair was blonde.

ART She's dyed her hair?

BEN No, in the dream. It was the same as yours, marble, sex, blondness.

ART Ben, you're exhausted.

BEN Are you going to bed now?

ART I'm having a brandy.

BEN Are you having a cigar?

ART Far too late for a cigar. (*Puffs, laughs to himself*) Are you alright?

BEN I'm fine — I just — I don't know, I was ringing to ask you something.

ART What is it, Ben?

BEN Don't dream about Catherine again.

ART Sure I never dream. That was a once-off.

BEN Where's Anne?

ART She's asleep.

BEN Are you going to wake her up?

ART No, it's too late. She always wakes when I get into bed.

BEN Talk to Anne, you'll feel better about it.

ART I feel fine — Is Catherine asleep?

BEN Why do you want to know?

21

ART Is she dreaming about me?

BEN I doubt it. She's just gone up. She always reads herself to sleep.

ART What's she reading?

BEN Some travel book — by your man who was drowned — a torpedo.

ART Did he drown?

BEN I believe he did. It's on the blurb anyway. Someone drowned at the end of some war.

ART Is it a good book?

BEN Well, Catherine's reading it.

ART Ages since I read a good book — Well, goodnight, Ben.

BEN Just don't dream — or dream about Anne, me, anyone except Catherine.

ART It's a coincidence though. I'm glad I was wild in her dream.

BEN Why?

ART I don't know. Out there I'm someone's fantasy man.

BEN You're not, you know.

ART Yeah, well, goodnight.

BEN And put out that cigar. I can smell it over the phone.

ART It's nearly finished.

BEN Are you going to pour another brandy?

ART I haven't thought that far ahead.

BEN I might have one, too. Don't feel like sleeping to-night. Isn't it ridiculous the way people go to bed every night? We're far too trusting — anything might happen.

ART Have a brandy, Ben, relax. 'Night.

BEN 'Night, Art.

> *He sits there a minute, takes a cigar from drawer, clippers, lights it, puffs, pours a drink.* ART *does the same in his space. They look at one another without seeing. And exit both.*

Scene Four

ANNE *comes on in coat and nightdress with takeaway coffee and paper and bag of croissants which she eats during this scene. Enter* ART *in suit, with briefcase, drinks her coffee, eats some of her croissant.*

ANNE What time did you come to bed last night?

ART Don't know. I sat in the garden. I saw the hare.

ANNE Yeah, she's back with two leverets.

ART I know. Raised my glass to them. Welcome to the world, little creatures, I said.

ANNE Did you? — You were talking in your sleep.

ART Did I wake you?

ANNE You were mourning with pleasure.

ART Mourning with pleasure?

ANNE Leave my croissants alone — you can get your own in town. Moaning — whatever it's called.

ART Did I say anything I should be ashamed of?

ANNE Lots.

ART I did not. I'm always on my best behaviour when asleep.

ANNE You look extremely guilty standing there in your suit.

ART I was born guilty — Kids are all fine?

ANNE Yeah, they're fine.

ART Are we all set for the Confirmation?

ANNE Communion.

ART That's right.

ANNE I'm getting caterers in. I can't be bothered anymore.

ART Well, don't look so sad about it. Are we inviting the world and its mother, or just our own ghastly shower?

ANNE Just our own ghouls.

ART All the crones?

ANNE Every last one of them.

ART Remind me to start on the wine early. Could we have a few friends? A few people we actually like?

ANNE Like who?

ART   Is there no one you like?

ANNE   Now that you ask, no, no one I like enough to put up with all day.

ART   What else was I saying in my sleep?

ANNE   I can't remember — sable or scrabble or — did you have a dream or something?

ART   I never dream.

ANNE   But last night?

ART   No — definitely no.

ANNE   I dreamt I was French kissing a dog. He was forcing my mouth open with his paws. He had my tongue clamped between his teeth.

ART   Was it good?

ANNE   And then you woke me up.

ART   With my mourning with pleasure.

ANNE   No, after that.

ART   What happened after that?

ANNE   You don't remember?

ART   No, what did I do?

ANNE   Don't look so frightened. You just made love to me.

ART   Last night?

ANNE   Towards morning.

ART   But that's impossible.

ANNE   What are you saying?

ART   I have no memory of it.

ANNE   Maybe you drank too much.

ART   I had two bottles of wine with dinner and four brandies. I don't think that's excessive. You must have been dreaming.

ANNE   I know when I'm being made love to.

ART   Maybe it was the dog. Well, I'm glad one of us had a good time.

ANNE   You enjoyed it, too.

ART   Did I?

ANNE   Your back was a river of sweat.

ART   And that equals enjoyment?

ANNE   (*Kisses him*) Darling, try and remember when you make love to me.

ART   I do. I usually do. This is bizarre.

ANNE Maybe you thought I was someone else — Look, if you ever need to have an affair, just go ahead — only don't tell me.

ART Why would I have an affair?

ANNE I'm just saying.

ART I'm not that kind of man. Why would I do a thing like that?

ANNE People do the strangest things.

ART In their thoughts maybe, but the waking world is different.

ANNE I don't find it so different. Recently I find the daylight strange, distorted, shadowy, where all was clear before.

ART Are you going to have an affair?

ANNE Not that I'm aware of.

ART Then why are you telling me to have one?

ANNE Just if you need to.

ART Are you tired of me?

ANNE I'm just tired, I'm tired of living. Of course I'm not tired of you.

ART Are you having an affair?

ANNE God, you're so literal. Just forget it. Forget it, Art. You're late.

ART I don't care if I'm late. I get no credit for being on time. What are you talking about?

ANNE Just breakfast conversation. I was so happy with you last night. Look, if you need to destroy us, do it without my knowing, that's all. I don't want honesty. I don't have the energy for honesty anymore.

ART What?

ANNE Go to work. We have lots of bills. Go to work.

ART I'll go in a minute.

ANNE Will I make a pot of coffee?

ART I don't want coffee — (*Drinking Anne's coffee*) What are you doing today?

ANNE What I always do.

ART What do you always do?

ANNE You know what I always do.

ART And what's in it for you?

ANNE You come home, the children are healthy, I'm alive.

ART That doesn't seem like much.

ANNE Lots survive on less. My life is full.

ART Have I been neglecting you?

ANNE Probably — Have you?

ART No, you have to tell me.

ANNE Tell you what? It's just living, Art. Just waiting for it all to end like everyone else.

ART I'd better go.

ANNE Do you want dinner or will I just eat with the children?

ART Can I call you later?

ANNE Don't leave it too late.

ART I won't.

Kisses her. And exit ART. ANNE *sits there eating croissants. And exits.*

Scene Five

Enter BEN *in a suit. Drinks from a bottle of water. He stands there looking out. Enter* ART *with a pile of papers, glasses, jacket over his arm.*

ART I've been all over the building — What're you doing up here?

BEN I like looking down on the city.

ART We've a meeting in five minutes. I thought you were meant to have this sorted.

BEN Fractions and decimals. Nothing to do with anything.

ART This is not the time for philosophy.

BEN Do you ever look down on this city? God bless us all is all I can say. You'd need to be made of steel and concrete to survive this place.

ART We are, Ben, we are — steel and concrete, decimals and fractions, the square root of nothing. But so what? So is everyone else.

BEN In time this will all be ice again. You know we're actually living in the middle of an ice age, always thought it was millions of years ago. The rising water is only the ice melting and when it's all melted it'll freeze again.

ART It's an ice-lolly world.

BEN Catherine dreamt about you again.

ART Did she?

BEN That's two dreams in forty-eight hours.

ART Was there marble in it?

BEN No, it was full of sand.

ART That's strange. I dreamt last night I was with Catherine on a beach, we were shipwrecked on this beach, and I kept thinking as I made love to her, I'm the one who's going to have to find water, build a hut, fight off natives, lions, scorpions, and night was coming on.

BEN Just what did you do to her?

ART I'm sorry, but I've done nothing — Did you dream?

BEN As a matter of fact I did have a dream last night.

ART About Anne?

BEN No, about you.

ART About me?

BEN You were prancing around in your underpants showing me the cherry blossom.

ART And was I a turn-on in my underpants?

BEN Smell the cherry blossom, you kept shrieking, and there were two cherry blossoms shedding, miraculously shedding in my garden. I have oaks in my garden, oaks for Christsakes, and there you are like some mad Cinderella waltzing round in your underpants, invading my lawn.

ART Suddenly I'm irresistible. Everyone's dreaming about me, even Anne — she said I made love to her last night.

BEN And didn't you?

ART I think she made it up.

BEN Maybe you thought Anne was Catherine and reached for her on your shipwrecked beach among the scorpions.

ART We're late. Let's get this meeting over with and take a long lunch.

BEN There's no time for lunch today — I hate my life.

ART (*Papers*) What's the story on this shower?

BEN Up to their necks in gutter. We don't go near them.

ART You better have your reasons. I hope you're in the mood for a row.

BEN Oh God, I'm going to die in a boardroom looking up some fella's hairy nostrils.

And exit both.

Scene Six

Enter CATHERINE *in nightdress with glass of wine and a child's story-book. A child cries offstage.*

CATHERINE Go to sleep now — good boy — I'll be up in a minute. (*Under her breath*) Oh Christ, give me a break!

Enter BEN.

BEN What's wrong with him?

CATHERINE He just won't settle. I've read him three stories.

BEN I'll go up.

CATHERINE Give him a minute, he might drop off.

BEN Does he cry every night?

CATHERINE Most nights, yes.

BEN It's pitiful.

CATHERINE After seventeen years of crying children you get pretty immune.

BEN Why is he crying?

CATHERINE Because he wants a chocolate bar and I wouldn't give him one, then he wanted me to cut my hair off and leave it on the pillow which I cruelly refused to do and then he wanted to paint his nails pink. But he's really crying because he can't make sense of this world and neither can his mother.

BEN *goes to her, kisses her.*

Did Art dream about me?

BEN On a tropical beach, no less.

CATHERINE What a cliché. I suppose we were happy.

BEN Ecstatic.

CATHERINE Is Art good-looking?

BEN I don't know.

CATHERINE Don't you have eyes?

BEN Not for men, no, I certainly don't.

CATHERINE   Describe him.

BEN   Art?

CATHERINE   Yeah.

BEN   He's an in-between man, I suppose. Not too bad, despite his cigars and his brandy. Eyes, wide spaced, dark, I think. Teeth are good, tans easily, veiny legs which he says he inherited from his mother, but his mouth is unfinished.

CATHERINE   What do you mean?

BEN   Foetal or something, like he's never been weaned.

CATHERINE   And your mouth?

BEN   I never got the breast. That's what's wrong with me. Rejection from day one. Were you thinking about him today?

CATHERINE   Yeah — can't stop.

BEN   It's really not on.

CATHERINE   Why isn't it on?

BEN   Well, there's me in the background.

CATHERINE   I think about you, too.

BEN   A lot?

CATHERINE   Enough.

BEN   And what do you think about when you think about me?

CATHERINE   What is this? The inquisition?

BEN   You're the one dreaming about people you shouldn't be.

CATHERINE   There is no vocabulary for this.

BEN   Do you want me to die?

CATHERINE   You're not exactly burning with life. Widows have a great time, it has to be said.

BEN   They do.

CATHERINE   All that freedom, no big man stomping round the kitchen rattling the knife drawer — Yeah, I'd like to be a girl again, without the stupidity, yes, I long to be alone, all this clutter is too much for me.

BEN   Have you dyed your hair?

CATHERINE   I set out the dye. I put on the gloves and then I said, what's the point? I suppose what I'm no longer capable of is deep feeling, you know, when

	your breath stops, except when I dream about Art. It's fantastic. Don't be jealous, Ben. I can't wait to go to sleep tonight and dream about him.
BEN	I wish you'd dream about me.
CATHERINE	But I'm not. I'm dreaming about Art and he's dreaming about me. Just who is it hurting?
BEN	Me.
CATHERINE	It's not. You can't control my mind. I can't control it. You can't tell me to switch off a dream just because it's not about you.
BEN	I don't have to like it.
CATHERINE	I think you should if it makes me happy.
BEN	I'm the one should make you happy.
CATHERINE	Don't be ridiculous.
BEN	So I'm just here taking up space?
CATHERINE	Well, yes, but that's normal.
BEN	What? Hovering with my hands in my pockets? Waiting for you to start the conversation? Sort out the day for me?
CATHERINE	Is that what you do? I suppose that's the way we go on. I hope Art dreams about me tonight. Michael got ninety-five in his reading. He told me to tell you, not to forget. Ring Art and tell him to dream about me tonight.
BEN	You're mad. I never realized it before.
CATHERINE	Well, *I* can't ring him.
BEN	Why not? You've such a fantastic time together.
CATHERINE	Anne might think I have designs on him.
BEN	And don't you?
CATHERINE	Only in bed, only in sleep.
BEN	I have a premonition of an impending catastrophe.
CATHERINE	A what?
BEN	A sentence from my English teacher. She made us write it down, she was talking about *Macbeth*. That's what I have, a premonition of an impending catastrophe.
CATHERINE	It's only a bit of distraction.
BEN	So if he stops dreaming about you it won't matter?
CATHERINE	He won't. We're too far in to just stop.

BEN Too far in?

CATHERINE I can't explain it. It's as if my real life is happening when I go to sleep and you and I are a dream, a fragment, difficult to remember on waking. Being awake is no longer important.

BEN But if he stops?

CATHERINE Don't say that to me.

BEN Why not?

CATHERINE You're tampering with the hard-wiring of my mind, my heart, my soul. Stop tampering with me.

BEN And you're playing with me. You like to see me jealous.

CATHERINE I didn't notice. Oh, Ben, it's the prose of living I can't take much longer. I look around me and everything irregular, irrational, opaque is what seems beautiful to me now. What are these senseless rules we live by? Who decided them and why? And the minute I assert any personality I'm rejected by you. Any whiff of the essential me is off. I'm so tired behaving myself.

BEN *goes to her, kisses her.*

BEN I wish you'd stop this nonsense and go back to your dreamless sleeps.

CATHERINE You like me catatonic.

BEN I like you to think about me.

CATHERINE 'Night.

And exit CATHERINE. BEN *wanders round, turning off lamp, tidying up. Exits.*

Scene Seven

Enter ART *with coffee in a takeaway cup, briefcase. He stands there a minute staring off into the distance.* BEN *walks by, briefcase, coffee, newspaper. Passes* ART *without a word.*

ART   Ben.

BEN   I see you.

ART   Stop. Stop for a minute.

BEN   You want to tell me about your fantastic dream?

ART   No dream.

BEN   You mean you're not going to tell me.

ART   No, I didn't dream about Catherine last night. I didn't dream at all.

BEN   Well, she dreamt about you.

ART   It'll stop soon.

BEN   She couldn't wait to wake and tell me.

ART   What was I doing?

BEN   The usual Romeo stuff under a marble statue, marble floor, white marble everywhere, and the pair of you sprawled all over it.

ART   If only it was real. I don't think I've ever been in a room with a white marble floor. You get all that fake stuff in hotel lobbies, but a real marble room, classical proportions, pillars, columns, statues that are not copies.

BEN   You dreamt it, too?

ART   Yeah, yeah, I dreamt it, too.

BEN   Then why did you lie?

ART   Because you look awful. Look, I don't give a hoot about Catherine. She's your wife so I want her to be okay so you're okay, but that's all, Ben, that's all.

BEN   Are you having an affair with Catherine?

ART   That's crazy.

BEN   No, listen, I've been thinking that all this dreaming is just a front, hiding the real thing that's going on.

ART   What real thing that's going on? Tell me. I'd love to know something real.

33

BEN You can't continue playing with me like this. Look, I've known you too long. If it's a big joke you've had your laugh, now come clean.

ART I'm not playing with you, Ben.

BEN Aren't you? Between the pair of you you've unhinged me. Catherine said last night that she'd like me to die.

ART She didn't. I don't believe that.

BEN And what was terrible was she was being philosophical about herself. She didn't mean to be cruel.

ART This is getting out of hand. Will I call Catherine?

BEN Don't you dare!

ART Alright. Christ!

BEN You're just looking for an excuse to be near her.

ART I am not.

BEN She's the same. She's fascinated with you. She can't stop herself talking about you. She loves saying your name.

ART So, what's that to do with me? I can't remember the last time I saw Catherine, spoke to her, I can't visualize her, she's blonde, right? Sandy blonde, darker in winter, blue eyes, is it? Or grey?

BEN I don't know.

ART You don't know the colour of your wife's eyes?

BEN They keep changing. Last night they were brown.

ART Has she dyed her hair yet?

BEN What's it to you? She's just a woman like any other. I can't see the individual in her, the space that defines her, that makes her who she is. I suppose I haven't thought about her in a long time and now, when I'm forced to look at her, she's not there, she's so strange all of a sudden.

ART Is it that you and Catherine are not happy and I'm being blamed? Piggy in the middle, gooseberry, the scapegoat who'll take the rap for everything?

BEN No, we're happy, we're happy, no more miserable than anyone else. There are children, gardens, afternoons looking out on the bay. All of that. We're not miserable, Art, far from it, but something has to

happen, you and Catherine have started something. I'm just the sleepwalker in the middle of it.

ART I refuse to take any responsibility if you and
Catherine break up.

BEN What are you talking about?

ART I'm just saying it now. I want no part in it. It has
nothing to do with me.

BEN You think you'll come out of this unscathed? We're
all in this. All of us.

ART Is that a threat?

BEN You think you can spill your sleeping world all
over me, all your hidden fantasies and passions, all
over my house, my wife, and walk away scot-free?

ART I thought we were friends.

BEN This is way beyond the call of friendship.

And exit BEN.

Scene Eight

ART *looks after* BEN. *Takes out his phone, clears his throat, dials.*
Enter ANNE. *Glass of wine, some crooner in the background.*

ANNE What is it, Art?

ART Can't I call you whenever I want?

ANNE But you never do. Is everything okay? (*Takes a sip of wine*)

ART Of course, a glorious morning. The sun is shining.

ANNE Don't talk to me about the sun. (*Looks out*) It goes on all day.

ART I'm drinking coffee in the plaza before I head into work.

ANNE Isn't that great for you?

ART   I just thought I'd ring to say hello.

ANNE What is it, Art? I'm busy.

ART You're always saying I never call you and when I do you have a go at me.

ANNE Has something happened?

ART No, nothing has happened. How are the kids?

ANNE They're fine, about their day.

ART And what are your plans for the day?

ANNE I'm going to the shop to buy digestive biscuits and washing-up liquid.

ART Have you noticed anything about me?

ANNE The cat's iris has fallen out.

ART Fuck the cat, have I changed?

ANNE She's staring at me through the window like it's my fault, with a hole in her eye. No, you haven't changed, do you want to change?

ART Of course not.

ANNE What is it, Art? What's wrong?

ART I just wanted to hear your voice.

ANNE Are you about to do something you shouldn't and you want me to say it's alright?

ART What would I be about to do?

ANNE God knows, I don't know, Art. I like to hear you, too.

ART But have you noticed anything odd in my behaviour this last while?

ANNE You're the same old Art, a bit more passionate these nights, but that's you, too.

ART Is it? Is that me?

ANNE Look, I can't tell you who you are, darling. I'm saving all vital energy for defining Anne, the several Annes that seem to have taken up residence in this old carcass. Don't worry, sweetheart, I'll be here this evening, one of me will, at any rate.

ART I never for a second suspected you wouldn't be there this evening. What in the name of God are you talking about?

ANNE Oh, Art, I'm just babbling on. Enjoy the day, darling, don't work too hard.

ART But there's something you're not saying.

ANNE Is there?

ART Yes, there is.

ANNE What? What have I forgotten?

ART That you love me.

ANNE Oh, that. I suppose I'm out of the habit.

ART But do you?

ANNE I don't like to be coerced into those three words. I'll tell you I love you if and when I feel like telling you.

ART It's impossible to have a romantic conversation with you! You think just because you have me in the bed you don't need to woo me out of it!

ANNE Is that what I think?

ART Yes, that's what you think! I know you, woman. You always think you know better.

ANNE Well, I'm glad you told me what I think. That's one thing off my list today. Thinking.

ART You're a contrary rip! Impossible to please, sitting on your fat arse, smug with sex.

ANNE I'm going to hang up now.

ANNE *hangs up and exits.*

ART That's right, hang up on me! Why can't you just say what you're supposed to say? I'll break you down yet. (*Flings the phone away*) That's the last time you get a romantic call from me.

>ART *picks up phone, straightens tie, preens himself, cuffs, jacket, briefcase. And exits.*

Scene Nine

Enter BEN. *The room is in shadow.*

BEN   Catherine? Catherine, are you here?

CATHERINE   (*A sigh*) Oh God — what?

BEN   Why is the house in darkness?

CATHERINE   I fell asleep — I was dreaming — I don't suppose you want to hear it.

BEN   Art has stopped dreaming about you.

CATHERINE   He hasn't!

BEN   He told me this morning he dreamt about another woman.

CATHERINE   Who?

BEN   What does it matter who? It wasn't you, that's the important thing.

CATHERINE   I don't believe it.

BEN   Can I turn the light on?

CATHERINE   No, I want shadow, candlelight, stars.

BEN   There are no stars here anymore — Just the lamp, then.

CATHERINE   Why must you always break the spell?

BEN   Is that what I do?

CATHERINE   You ruin every dusk. And when it's dark you ruin the dark. Why did you tell me Art dreamt about me in the first place, only to take it from me?

BEN   I'm sorry. I should never have told you.

CATHERINE   You actually believe you're innocent, wronged, that Art and I are the deviants?

BEN   And aren't you?

CATHERINE   That was my lifeline!

BEN   Art dreaming about you?

CATHERINE   I didn't think I needed one but now you've taken it I feel I'm being sucked up out of here. I live for sleeping, dreaming about Art, my waking life is just pretence.

BEN   Well, of course it is, Catherine. It is for everyone.

CATHERINE   I don't care about everyone. The same for everyone!

What about me? Me? I am here now, in time, for a very, very short time, and I doubt I will ever be again. Why this thing called me if every avenue of expression is closed off from me? And all I have to look forward to is dying?

BEN There are codes and rules and contracts we must live by, Catherine. And as for dying we are dying all the time — Look at this hand, the skin on it is dead, look at your face, the skin on your cheeks died yesterday. Ridiculous to think, monumentally stupid, to hope it all just happens at the end.

CATHERINE And love?

BEN An awful repetition of nights and days and days and nights.

CATHERINE Please, Ben, tell me, has he really stopped?

BEN No — I made it up — I just want — Just want all of this to be over.

CATHERINE It is over. I've crossed some line or other without realizing it. And it's fantastic, Ben, something is happening to me.

Lights down.

ACT TWO

Scene One

ART *sits at table drinking a glass of red wine and smoking a cigar.*
Enter CATHERINE *with a glass of red wine.*

CATHERINE   Art?

ART   My God! I was just thinking about you, was thinking how lovely it would be if I bumped into you.

CATHERINE   You were not! — And here I am.

ART   And here you are.

CATHERINE   Ben's not here, is he?

ART   No, he won't have a glass with me these days.

CATHERINE   Well, I will.

> *She sits.*

Cheers. (*They clink glasses*)

ART   Why are you here?

CATHERINE   I got a babysitter. I went to the art gallery. I thought
I might run into Ben. No, I wanted to be on my
own — I just wanted to have a look at you.

ART   And how was the gallery?

CATHERINE   A blur — a blur of relentless colour — drank it all
in too quickly, feel dizzy now, like there are moths
fluttering and banging around my brain. I stood in
front of this painting, can't remember who it was,
but a woman just staring out at me with dirty
fingernails, one of the Dutch maybe, and I wished
I could be her, fixed in a painting somewhere,
trapped behind glass. And people could come and
stare and think what they liked about me and it
wouldn't matter. My expression wouldn't change,

my dress would still be green, my hands filthy.

ART And what do you think of me? Do I disappoint?

CATHERINE Your neck is a bit — I don't know —

ART What's wrong with my neck?

CATHERINE Well, it's a bit — Thought it was longer — It's hardly a neck at all. There's nothing wrong with your neck.

ART This is the real world, baby. Some people are neckless here. No marble around to glisten off.

CATHERINE I must be a fright to look at?

ART Let me tell you something, Catherine. You are exactly as I dream you. Ben said your hair was brown.

CATHERINE I dyed it.

ART For me?

CATHERINE For the dream. For me. Yes, for you. I want to be that dream. I want to live it. I want it to be my waking world.

ART And Ben?

CATHERINE Oh, Ben, Ben, Ben. What is Ben at?

ART Ben loves you.

CATHERINE Ben loves the idea of me. He doesn't know the first thing about me.

ART And I do?

CATHERINE Describe to me the dream you had last night.

ART No.

CATHERINE Why not?

ART It seems ridiculous now.

CATHERINE You believe in the day too much.

ART The day is where we must live.

CATHERINE I disagree. Night is where it all happens.

ART In a million years perhaps, but not now. This is the age of ice, an era when men's and women's hearts were frozen. That's how they'll describe us in the future. But we can't live in the future. It has been given to us now, this age of prose and flint and it is here, just here, we must bide our time.

CATHERINE No, no, Art, you mustn't talk like that. You know I've been looking around this last while, I've been looking at people a lot, and I see us all now as some fabulous species, and you know something, Art, it is we who are the beautiful thing, yes us, not God, not mountains, oceans, rivers, architecture, none of that haphazard vastness, but us, wandering through this hostile landscape, so full of hope, for what? And despair, for why?

ART   It's what we do, Catherine. It's called living. It happens to everyone.

CATHERINE   This blinding joy?

ART   Moments. Yes.

CATHERINE   I know I don't seem like a great prospect right now, but that's because I've spent all these years cutting bits of myself off. With you — I would retrieve them.

ART   Catherine — that is not possible.

CATHERINE   You get enough just dreaming?

ART   Well, no — but —

CATHERINE   Anne — the children.

ART   Yes — all of that.

CATHERINE   You coward — you're using me.

ART   How am I using you?

CATHERINE   You deny me now? Last night I was sprawled under you.

ART   You were not.

CATHERINE   Ben told you to say the dreams have stopped.

ART   They have.

CATHERINE   You're afraid. Don't be. It's me, Art. I'm afraid, too. But what awaits us if we would only —

ART   I can't, Catherine.

CATHERINE   Look, I have a whole show on the road, too. You think I come to you on a whim? I know the fallout for Ben and the children will be terrible.

ART   I have a wife I wouldn't hurt for the world. I have four children.

CATHERINE   I know how many children you have.

ART   I have a good life. You have, too. Ben is a good man.

CATHERINE   I am so sick of being told I have a good life. That I have a good man, that my children are beautiful. I'm not denying any of it and I'm not ungrateful and may the gods not strike me down, but I want more. I want more than good. I want spectacular. I want marble, marble, marble.

ART Last night was spectacular.

CATHERINE So you don't deny it?

ART I don't deny it, but how do we get from here to there? It's the coldness of this world I can't take, the terrifying greyness that saturates my days and nights. Half the time I look up at the sky, when I remember to, and it's just not there, only a cloak of elephant iron weighing me down where that indigo should be and, you know, sometimes I think our dreaming is about dying, that I don't care to prolong the jaunt much further here.

CATHERINE Then let it be about dying. It's happening anyway.

ART You're dangerous.

CATHERINE Am I?

ART You want destruction, don't you?

CATHERINE Anything new seems to involve it. There can be no change without change.

ART Change is what I do not want.

CATHERINE You think I want it? It would be far easier for me to stay with my good life, my good man, my beautiful children.

ART Then stay.

CATHERINE And give up, is it?

ART It's what everyone does.

CATHERINE So like sheep we should do the same?

ART Yes, exactly the same.

CATHERINE So what you're saying is there is no place in this world for our dream of marble.

ART You assume too much. A handful of dreams. How can they possibly impact here? Where is the place for them?

CATHERINE In our hearts. There is nowhere else.

ART Just because you know me intimately in that marble room you shouldn't presume anything out of it. I am, or rather was, your husband's oldest friend.

CATHERINE Don't lecture me on loyalty. I know the cost of what

	we're talking about.
ART	What *you're* talking about.
CATHERINE	I know the price that will be extracted in blood. Your blood. Mine. I have thought this through. I don't sit here talking to you lightly. I don't ask you to come with me lightly.
ART	I'm going nowhere with you. (*Gets up*) I'm going home. If you're wise you'll say nothing to Ben about this.
CATHERINE	I'm past protecting anyone, least of all myself. Don't go. Have another glass with me.
ART	I have to go.
CATHERINE	You're afraid of me.
ART	Yes, I am.
CATHERINE	I am, too. Feel like a lone magpie on the wind, a bad omen, sorrow for everyone around me, so be it.
ART	Goodnight, Catherine, and don't say anything to Ben. He'll read it all wrong.
CATHERINE	You're more worried about Ben than anything.
ART	I am. I just can't do this. It's not I'm not tempted but there are laws — unwritten, but there nevertheless.
CATHERINE	Your laws are crippling.
ART	That may be so but they're all that's between us and chaos. For the third time, goodnight.

And exit ART. CATHERINE *sits there looking after him. Takes stub of his cigar from ashtray, smells it. Holds it. Sips from his unfinished wine. And exits.*

Scene Two

Enter BEN *with sandwich and coffee, sits, begins opening sandwich, forgets about it, stares out. Enter* ART *after a minute. Stops, looks at* BEN.

ART Are you avoiding me?

BEN Damn right I am.

ART I was wondering if you'd care to go fishing on Saturday or Sunday?

BEN I work. I go home. That's it now.

ART Is she improving?

BEN Sleeps all day.

ART So who's looking after the kids?

BEN No one. She sits like a statue at the kitchen table and they tiptoe round her.

ART Dare I ask?

BEN Yes, the dreams keep coming and coming.

ART Yeah.

BEN You're still dreaming about her?

ART Yes, I suppose I am.

BEN You never stopped.

ART So? It's nothing, Ben.

BEN Why don't you just fuck her and be done with it. Run away with her. It'd be over in a week.

ART You're blaming me for all of this.

BEN Just for your part in it.

ART Ever occur to you it's you wants everything to change? It's you wants rid of Catherine?

BEN I am not the dreamer here.

ART And suppose I do go off with her, what then?

BEN I don't know, build your marble room, frolic in it till ye suffocate, tear it down around ye. Puncture your wild fantasies.

ART And what of your wild fantasies?

BEN There are none.

ART Everyone has them.

BEN Mine are darkness and silence.

ART   I don't believe you.

BEN   That's the official version. My private life is my private life. I don't spew it over the first passerby.

ART   Well, if you believe I would walk into your house and just steal your woman you don't know me.

BEN   No, I don't know you. I begin to realize I don't know anyone.

ART   We're dealing with elusive territory, Ben, things imagined, without rhyme or reason. You and Catherine are confusing the two worlds, trying to apply there to here. And trying to hold me to ransom because of it. I am not responsible for my dreams. They're just visitors, uninvited, come and go as they please.

BEN   She says your spirits meet in this marble room.

ART   So? So what? So they meet?

BEN   Easy for you to say. I have a woman at home who sleeps twenty-four hours a day, she gets up in the middle of the night, eats crackers and hard-boiled eggs from their shells which she scatters around the carpets, the stairs. She hovers around windows, doorways, leans against the fence for an hour at a time, and then sinks back into her catatonic dream of you.

ART   I can't help you, Ben. I can't help Catherine. I have my own circus, children in school, a wife I love. I'm not throwing that away for —

BEN   Do you love Anne? You don't look to me like a man in love.

ART   And you do?

BEN   Nothing bears scrutiny, does it? I told you at the start how it would be. You laughed in my face, lit another cigar, sloshed down more brandy. You leather-skinned slobs who dribble and drool over other people's lives, smearing and sundering without even realizing, all the time pleading innocence. Well, I'm sorry, but that sort of blundering innocence is a crime. She is pining for you. She's skin and bone, she is very fragile right now, and you treated her so callously.

ART She told you then?

BEN How dare you treat my wife like that! You dare to get on your high moral horse with her when you started the whole thing.

ART I was very reasonable with her. What do you want from me, Ben? Are you asking me to have an affair with her?

BEN Yes — I believe I am.

ART Maybe it's you wants the affair with me?

BEN Is that what you think?

ART The whole thing is so out of control I don't know what to think anymore.

BEN Well, be assured on one point. I have no desire to have anything to do with you. I want my wife back. Look, I'm feeding and dressing a woman who no longer loves me and now I wonder if she ever has. I want her back. And if I have to give her to you to get her back, then that's what I have to do.

ART That is never going to happen.

BEN I'm afraid she's going to die on me! We're dealing with hearts and minds here, Art, mine and Catherine's, not some after dinner titillation. I knew you'd run when the chips were down.

ART I'm protecting my own hearth is all.

BEN I should ring Anne, tell her the lie of the land.

ART Leave Anne out of this. I don't want her sullied with this. I don't want this near my house.

BEN This is what thirty years' friendship comes down to.

ART Don't threaten me with Anne.

BEN But Catherine is fair game?

ART I am so sorry, Ben, if I have been careless.

BEN Careless?

ART Yes, careless! That's all it was. I am sorry but for you to attack my wife because of a lapse in me is despicable. That's what cowards do, go after the women and children.

BEN And what of my woman and my children?

ART Not in my house! This is your mess. Catherine's

mess. Don't bring it near my lair.

BEN It's already there.

ART What have you done?

BEN I don't need to do anything. Look at you.

And exit BEN. ART *stands there a minute, shaken, recovers his composure, then exits.*

Scene Three

Sound of ANNE, *off.*

ANNE   Come in. Come in. Honestly. Once I answer the door I let people in.

CATHERINE   What a lovely hall.

ANNE   Of course I never have visitors.

CATHERINE   (*Entering, followed by* ANNE) I don't either. I hope you don't think it odd of me just dropping in without calling first.

ANNE   It's very odd. You're lucky I wasn't napping.

CATHERINE   How are you?

ANNE   Keeping going, keeping going.

CATHERINE   Yes, I can see you're keeping going with that bright smile on your face.

ANNE   Is it bright, my smile? Well, it was the smile I was given or maybe I learned it along the way. Will I make tea? Wine? Coffee?

CATHERINE   I brought you these. (*Flowers*)

ANNE   No, keep them for yourself.

CATHERINE   Well, they're dead. I certainly don't want them. Why do people bring dead things to one another?

ANNE   Look, I've enough rubbish in my life. It's a lovely thought, though.

CATHERINE   I don't suppose you heard I've been — I don't know — not myself anyway.

ANNE   You look fine to me.

CATHERINE   But I'm not, despite the lipstick and the new shawl and trousers — I'm very far from myself right now.

ANNE   Yes, Art told me. Ben is very worried about you.

CATHERINE   Feel I've been peeled like an onion. I'm down to the core and there's nothing there.

ANNE   There's breathing.

CATHERINE   Moss breathes. Cement breathes.

ANNE   As long as you're breathing there's something going on.

CATHERINE   But the mind, the heart, the soul, whatever it is

that's me is just not there. Maybe it never was. I
am far more than just breath.

ANNE No, you're not. None of us are. You're smoke. A
light breeze will blow you away.

CATHERINE You're one of those old cynics.

ANNE I just don't expect anything. I live by ritual, repetition. This old machine thrives on cappuccinos and
emptying the dishwasher and polishing my white
marble tiles in the hall. I'm in love with those tiles.
I made Art import them.

CATHERINE Yes, I noticed them.

ANNE I love the sheen, the light, the texture and grain.

CATHERINE And that's enough for you?

ANNE I do have a few other things, of course, to disguise
the journey.

CATHERINE Like what?

ANNE Am I boring you?

CATHERINE No, tell me.

ANNE Well, I have half a bottle of red wine in the evening.
Every evening. I think I would murder someone if
I couldn't have my three glasses of red wine in the
evening. I measure them out. Generous measures.
And I have a cigarette with each glass. I'm not a
fascist about the cigarettes but I must have the
wine. No one, but no one, can interfere with that.

CATHERINE It's very — I don't know what.

ANNE Yes, I refuse to panic.

CATHERINE What else do you do?

ANNE I read to the children.

CATHERINE Everyone does that. That's nothing to sustain you.
Even I read to the children.

ANNE And something a lot of people don't realize and forget to do and become depressed or psychopaths,
but I figured out years ago.

CATHERINE What?

ANNE I leave the lights on all day in winter, lamps, over-
head lights, every light blazing in the house, all
winter.

CATHERINE Your battle against the dark.

ANNE   Pathetic I know but I need to. It keeps me — I suppose it keeps me here.

CATHERINE   So you refuse darkness, you deny it. Do you sleep with the lights blazing?

ANNE   Until Art comes to bed. Then I don't mind if they're off.

CATHERINE   He's like a lamp, is he?

ANNE   And every morning I decide what time I'll go to bed at. Before I get up I'll say to myself, okay, tonight bedtime is at ten for you, missus, or nine or eleven. It's a matter of light policing of myself, not engaging because I've long figured out there's nothing there to engage with. Just a simple police state. At the appointed hour I do this or that and so time does not encroach on me or weigh me down or disturb me in any way.

CATHERINE   Is my visit disturbing you?

ANNE   There is room for the unplanned, up to a point.

CATHERINE   This is what Art is married to. What Art comes home to in the evening, kisses goodbye in the morning. This is what Art is so desperate to hold onto.

ANNE   I'm past caring how I appear. As long as it keeps me off window ledges.

CATHERINE   You like window ledges?

ANNE   What woman doesn't? It's one of the big themes, isn't it?

CATHERINE   So seductive to fly off one.

ANNE   The will I, won't I, thrill of it.

CATHERINE   And do you dream?

ANNE   Why?

CATHERINE   Because I do.

ANNE   Other people's dreams don't interest me.

CATHERINE   Not even if they're about your husband?

ANNE   You dream about Art?

CATHERINE   I can't stop.

ANNE   Oh.

CATHERINE   Erotic dreams, like a drug.

ANNE   You can't have him.

CATHERINE	So you own him?
ANNE	I surely do.
CATHERINE	He's part of your police state?
ANNE	The chief superintendent. I'd rather you didn't dream about him.
CATHERINE	So would everyone.
ANNE	It's time for my wine. (*Pours*) Do you want a glass?
CATHERINE	Only if it doesn't interfere with your quota.
ANNE	I have cases of it.

Hands her a glass of wine. CATHERINE *takes it, wanders around.* ANNE *lights a cigarette, watches her.*

	It's messy. There are cobwebs and I don't wash windows or floors, gave that up a few years ago. I'm a housewife who does no housework.
CATHERINE	There are a lot of us. (*Photo*) Is that one of your sons?
ANNE	That's Art. That's what he looked like when I met him. I took it. He'd just caught his first salmon of the season.
CATHERINE	He's so beautiful.
ANNE	(*Looks at photo*) Yeah — he was.
CATHERINE	Can I have it?
ANNE	Just because I give you a glass of wine doesn't mean you can bare your soul to me. I hate confessions. I can't stand them.
CATHERINE	I would like this photograph. I could get a copy made and return it to you. And since I've lost all my pride asking you I think you should give it to me.
ANNE	I don't like to see people without their pride — Take it then — as a loan.
CATHERINE	Thank you. (*She puts it in her bag*)
ANNE	Would you like a cigarette?
CATHERINE	I don't smoke.
ANNE	Is there anything else you want?
CATHERINE	Your life. I'll just drink this and go.
ANNE	What is it?

CATHERINE Oh, you don't want to know.

ANNE You came to tell me something.

CATHERINE Did I?

ANNE I thought you were a missionary at the door before I recognized you. You want to convert me to something.

CATHERINE I had something to say but it seems appalling now in front of your wholesome decency.

ANNE My wholesome decency?

CATHERINE I don't mean it as an insult, or maybe I do. I don't know anymore, but you've read the book on etiquette. You're too civilized for me.

ANNE What else is there?

CATHERINE There's more, believe me, there's more.

ANNE Like what?

CATHERINE No, you're too innocent, too decent. You've it all planned to your grave. I wish I had a grave plan, a scheme that would take me to the end without my noticing. I should congratulate you on the ingenious scaffolding you hang about yourself to evade time which is really just another name for emptiness. Oh the emptiness, the emptiness, to die of an empty heart must surely be a crime. Here (*photo*), take this back. I don't know how I could've asked for it.

ANNE Keep it. It's nothing.

CATHERINE It's not nothing. It's your husband.

ANNE That's not him. He's as dead to me in that photo as someone from the eleventh century.

CATHERINE And is he alive for you now? As he is now?

ANNE What an odd question.

CATHERINE He is dreaming about me.

ANNE So that's what's wrong with him. That's all. Thank God. I thought he had cancer and wasn't telling me.

CATHERINE You don't believe in the finer things, do you? The subtle things that quicken the blood and quiver the knee?

ANNE Oh, I believe in them, too much to ever mention them. My motto now is keep the head down, stay

CATHERINE   out of trouble, hold fast to those you need and who need you.

CATHERINE   I used to be like that, too.

ANNE   I know it's not living on the edge but there isn't room on the edge for everyone. Countries have to be run, children fed, taxes paid, all the stuff the drones take care of while you lost little wisps have your crises. Art belongs here. You can't have him. He is necessary for my life and my children's lives to run smoothly, without event or upset.

CATHERINE   So you decide everything for Art?

ANNE   Always have. Is it not that way for everyone else?

CATHERINE   No, it's not.

ANNE   They just don't realize it yet.

CATHERINE   No, there's a percentage, dwindling yes, but a number nevertheless who believe in the individual and the individual's rights and choices and responsibilities.

ANNE   The only individuals I know are in mental hospitals or remote rural parts of the country which are really just open asylums. Do you want to end up there? Drugged to the eyeballs, weeping for having crossed the line?

CATHERINE   Is that what you're afraid of?

ANNE   Crossing the line? To be sure I am. And let me tell you something, Catherine, you can cross as many lines as you want but I won't let you take Art with you. You'd probably survive. He won't. Just what do you expect? For me to hand him to you on a platter?

CATHERINE   Not quite, but I didn't expect such fierce holding on to someone you no longer love.

ANNE   Leave love out of it. It's about deals, deals between strangers. There's your definition of love. (*Pours wine*) You want another glass?

CATHERINE   No, I'll go. Just one thing. Whatever I am, a blunderer, a fool, I am not heartless. You're the heartless one, talking about yourself and Art like that. You are people, you are here, you will never be again.

How can you be so hard on him? How can you be so terrible to yourself?

ANNE   And Ben?

CATHERINE   Ben is none of your business. This has nothing to do with Ben. This is between Art and me. It was stupid of me to come.

And exit CATHERINE.

Scene Four

BEN *wanders around the room, hands in his pockets. After a while enter* CATHERINE *in coat and scarf, handbag.*

CATHERINE Oh, you're up.

BEN You were staying out until I'd gone to bed?

CATHERINE Something like that — yeah.

BEN I decided to sit up all night, wander the rooms like you, see would it throw light on anything.

CATHERINE We are not an equation to be solved.

BEN One thing has occurred to me, traipsing the house.

CATHERINE The wisdom of the night.

BEN For some time now I suppose we have passed the point where anything new can happen to us.

CATHERINE Long passed it.

BEN This city is grey and brown, not the colours of possibility. The odd patch of green in public spaces, usually locked, our garden perhaps, but really there is no refuge from the inevitable, no softening, no buffer anymore.

CATHERINE No, there isn't.

BEN We must rear our young until they can survive without us. And that's it. The life pared back to the essentials. Sooner or later it comes down to this.

CATHERINE It's not enough.

BEN Is it not?

CATHERINE You know it isn't.

BEN There's travel.

CATHERINE I have lost the capacity to walk the pavements of other people's cities. I can't even walk my own anymore.

BEN Come here.

CATHERINE No, you'll only kiss me.

BEN Then I'll come to you.

He does, takes her in his arms.

CATHERINE Don't kiss me.

He does, a long passionate kiss.

BEN Was that so terrible?
CATHERINE We've done this a million times, what does it alter?
— There's nothing wrong with your kisses.
BEN Which means there's nothing right with them —
With this body I thee worship — Remember that?
CATHERINE I wanted to run down the aisle.
BEN You think I didn't?
CATHERINE I wish you'd find someone else.
BEN You don't.
CATHERINE I do. I swear. You need someone who believes in
all of this. I need to be alone now with myself. I
need to leave while I still love you, before it all
turns ugly.
BEN What?
CATHERINE You heard me.
BEN Just like that?
CATHERINE Nothing happens just like that. It swells and swells
inside until one day you make a decision, prob-
ably the wrong one, but just to decide something.
Hopefully it will lead on to — somewhere else.
BEN To Art?
CATHERINE No, no — Art despises me.
BEN And I should comfort you because Art despises
you?
CATHERINE I was so wrong about Art. I don't know why he is
still such a huge presence inside me — maybe he's
just a signal, a beacon, not important in himself
but a sign that has brought me to a different place
— strange that, and I thought he was the great
magic thing that has been missing.
BEN And the children?
CATHERINE Don't mention the children. Please. I've done my
time. I'm no good for them anymore. You must
keep them safe now.
BEN And what will you do?

CATHERINE I will sit in a chair or stand looking out a window until the end comes. I won't force it but neither will I stop it.

BEN What is happening to you? Why are you talking like this?

CATHERINE I'm about to take a dive, Ben, a dive down into the dark, the blue, blue dark. I know I won't return but if I do I will be altered beyond recognition. If you're wise you'll let me remove myself from you and the children, let me just flounder down there.

BEN These dreams of marble that won't stop coming. I've been thinking about them, and all I can think of are those marble beds we lie under when we die. Is that what you want? A marble bed? And to be under it, not over, because you won't in this world and probably not in the next. A marble bed, all its weight fastening you down, glinting dimly under star and moon but mostly dull, weed-strangled, forgotten. Is that what you want, Catherine? Someone who cannot be brought back here? Never to be whole again?

CATHERINE Do you believe, actually believe, this sojourn here means something?

BEN Yes, I do. If it doesn't then there is nothing, nothing to hold on to.

CATHERINE Houses, jobs, children, art galleries, theatres, stadiums, wine bars, trees, mountains, birds, for God's sake, who can possibly believe in the fact of a bird?

BEN Yes, I believe in all of those things, Catherine. We are surrounded by mystery, glutted with it, so much so we must deny it all to go on.

CATHERINE They believed it in Babylon, too, and there is no trace of them now. I walk this city and all I see is scaffolding, building, building, building, an avalanche of warrens and rat holes to stuff us in, and all I can think of is Troy. And when people ask me for directions in the street I have to turn away quickly so I don't laugh in their faces. How can they possibly stand there with a map when everything is in such chaotic flux? But they point with their mortal fingers, insisting that such and such a place actually exists to be visited and admired or criticized. Turn left, I say, always left, when what I really want to tell them is, there will be no trace of you or I or that child you hold so lovingly by the hand, a hundred years from now there will be no trace of us, not a whisper, not a puff of ether, we're gone, we were never born.

BEN   You're not well, really you're not.

CATHERINE   I'm just talking, Ben, about my life. It's not pretty but it's mine. This is what is happening to me.

BEN   It is not yours. It is mine, too. It's the children's. You cannot talk like this in our house. I won't permit it. This guffawing at innocent strangers whose only crime is to ask you directions. It's barbaric, Cath-erine. It is barbaric.

CATHERINE   Yes, it is. My reptilian brain is on the ascent, and I'm on a descent, a descent away from some marble room that cannot be reached. Why are we given such images, such sublime yearnings for things that are never there? A dream was given to me, inside me from birth, a dream of marble, a woman in a marble room with her lover. And all the waking world can do is thwart it and deny it, and say, no, it cannot be, childish, impossible, you must walk the grey paths with the rest of us, go down into the wet muck at the close. That's your lot. That's what you have to look forward to. Well, I refuse it, Ben, I refuse it. I refuse this grey nightmare with its ridiculous rules and its lack of primary colours. And I despise you for lying down under it, worse, for embracing it, for being so smug, satisfied with so little.

BEN   You think I'm satisfied?

CATHERINE   You're not champing at the bit.

BEN   If I'm not champing at the bit it's because I know the wilderness is out there, and that we are safe inside seems to me a great miracle. That we are run of the mill, escaping all the terrible things that living can bestow or withhold. Why court tragedy? Why bring it into our nest? Why speak with such disdain against those who love you most?

CATHERINE Because I need the wilderness now.

BEN You realize what you're saying cannot be unsaid?

CATHERINE I realize it.

BEN There will be no reconciliation if you walk out that door.

CATHERINE The price is high — ferocious.

BEN What'll I say to the children?

A long pause.

CATHERINE Whatever you need to.

BEN But where will you go?

CATHERINE God knows. I might disappear off the face of the earth tonight, that's how insubstantial I feel right now — I'm just going to get a few things together. I'll take some money, too. Is that alright?

BEN I don't believe this is happening.

CATHERINE It seems to be — I don't want to talk to you anymore or I'll waver. I'll just look at the children and then — gone.

And exit CATHERINE. BEN *stands there looking after her.*

Scene Five

Enter ART *with brandy and cigar.* ANNE *enters, sits reading and sipping wine.* ART *wanders the space, watching her.*

ART Is it good?

ANNE Riveting.

ART What's it about?

ANNE This woman who is having an affair with her son.

ART Do people still do that?

ANNE People do everything.

ART Except us.

ANNE It's set in France, exotic, kind of high-class incest. It happens between the croissants and the boeuf bourguignon and the Veuve Cliquot. More palatable, I suppose.

ART You'd marvel at their energy, all that passion. I don't read anymore but there was an article in the paper today —

ANNE Don't tell me, something about what a happy little nation we are, a woman in a bikini telling us to invest so we'll be happier.

ART No, this was about the nuclear family. It's over.

ANNE Of course it is. Too much has to be excluded for it to survive.

ART I suppose.

ANNE It's a throwback, like believing in God.

ART Do you believe in God?

ANNE No one asks that question anymore apparently.

ART I'm asking it.

ANNE I saw a red sofa today.

ART Do we need another sofa?

ANNE It's just something to do. Order it. Pay for it. It won't arrive for six months by which time we'll have forgotten about it. I'd like to put it in the hall instead of that table.

ART Then do.

ANNE But where will I put the table?

ART You know what, Anne? I don't give a damn where you put the table.

ANNE And what do you give a damn about?

ART Right now, another brandy.

ANNE You should eat out more. I see far too much of you.

ART I've no one to eat out with.

ANNE What's wrong with Ben?

ART Ben is having a breakdown.

ANNE Catherine was here today.

ART What was she doing here?

ANNE Haven't a clue. She looked fantastic — hollowed out, on fire with something. Whatever's wrong with her it suits her.

ART She has no business here.

ANNE Are you afraid of her or something?

ART I hardly know the woman.

ANNE Yeah, well, ferocity coming off her in waves, felt helpless in front of her, that she would take my life and trample on it if let. She was admiring your photograph.

ART Was she?

ANNE She wanted it.

ART And you said no.

ANNE No, I gave it to her.

ART Don't give my photograph to people.

ANNE Why not?

ART Just don't. It's dangerous.

ANNE What's wrong with you these days?

ART Why don't you have some more wine, a brandy, knock yourself out?

ANNE Is that what you're doing?

ART I don't like to be too sober in the evening.

ANNE Thank God for that.

ART I wish something would happen to us — to me.

ANNE Something good?

ART Of course something good. No one seems to know who they are in this house.

ANNE That's why I want that sofa.

ART So you can concentrate on the sofa's faults.

ANNE It's not even beautiful. I'm sick of it already. I bought it anyway.

ART Then why ask my opinion?

ANNE I want you to believe you are considered in the matter of sofas in your hall.

ART So we can leave all the visitors in the hall?

ANNE What visitors?

ART Is it that bad?

ANNE We're under siege. Haven't you noticed? My God, you're so dim.

ART Am I?

ANNE Say something interesting or I'll have to go to bed. Just write the day off like all the yesterdays and all the tomorrows. Tell me a story.

ART I have no stories.

ANNE Make one up.

ART About what? — Okay, here's a story for you. Once there was a man, happily married, big house, good-looking wife, healthy children. He made enough not to have to worry.

ANNE About sofas.

ART His wife bought five sofas every day. There wasn't room to move with all the sofas. Then one night it struck this man that all these sofas were a trap, a banal trap. His wife sat opposite him on her new sofa. He sat opposite her on his new sofa. We're death sitting opposite one another on designer sofas, the man said.

ANNE To himself.

ART Of course, to himself. He was a businessman, he didn't deal in metaphors. He didn't read, didn't listen to music, go to the theatre, the opera, he was past all of that and grown coarse with its passing, though in his youth he had loved distraction, more than distraction, to fill himself up with all the good and necessary things. All that was left was fishing. So he went fishing but the salmon he caught was seeping green and cancerous because the river was over and the ocean was silted up. So he threw the salmon back into the filthy water and never went fishing again. Now what's left, the man wondered, as he sank into another new sofa and drank a brandy from another new brandy glass and smoked an ever more expensive cigar. There is nothing left, he said to himself as he watched his good-looking wife read a story about tasteful incest. He went to bed thinking he could die that night and it wouldn't matter. But instead of dying he had a dream. He dreamt he was in a room full of marble and on the marble bed was a beautiful woman, her hair was spun gold, her eyes were a turquoise grey, her throat was smooth and white as the marble pillar she leaned upon. He lay beside her on the gleaming bed, the veins in her arms running like the crystal blue rivers of Eden. How have I come from nothing to this, the man marvelled, from nothing to this awesome soul breathing beside me? She leaned on one marble elbow and ran a finger across his lips. You have come to this place of marble, the woman said, because you have asked. And then he woke.

ANNE   And then what happened?

ART   Then the man got up and left the room, left his sleeping wife, his children, his sofas, his brandy, his expensive cigars, and he went and found the marble woman who lived not far. He went into her marble room and they lay down together and wept. That they should be so happy. That they should cause such suffering to the good-looking wife and the good husband and the healthy children and all the sofas. But even so they vowed to one another that they would stay in the marble room together forever.

ANNE   So.

ART   (*Phone, laptop, briefcase, puts on jacket*) Do you know where my overcoat would be?

ANNE   What do you want an overcoat for in this weather?

ART   It'll be winter soon.

ANNE It won't work out like that, Art.

ART I have to leave because you won't.

ANNE Why should I?

ART You want to be the martyr, the abandoned one.

ANNE You're not leaving me for a mere dream of marble. Did you even dream it?

ART I certainly did.

ANNE Who is she?

ART I have no idea.

ANNE That Catherine.

ART I've hardly spoken three words to her in as many years. But, yes, I'm going to ask her to come with me.

ANNE You would do that to Ben?

ART I'm beyond loyalty.

ANNE To me? To your children?

ART Yes, I would do that.

ANNE I should shout and scream, hit you across the face. I can't muster up the wherewithal. Go. Go. Go. You're braver than me. And don't come back. You'll end up under an archway.

ART I may.

ANNE The other won't happen.

ART You don't know what'll happen when I walk out that door. Sure as hell nothing happening here.

ANNE That at least is true. Go on then. Let me see you walk out that door.

ART Can't we part amicably? This is so predictable.

ANNE You must be joking.

ART Right so. Take me to the cleaners. Use the children as weapons.

ANNE I aim to.

ART This is our love in a nutshell. This is what it comes down to at the toss of a coin. The great happy marriage.

ANNE It surprises you? That it's a fiction? An empty fiction? The dogs in the street know that much. Step out of line and the sky falls in, glance sideways for a second and it's gone. Don't look so hurt. Go. Go on. Go to your brilliant future, your marble fantasy.

ART I will. I'll head in that general direction.

ANNE You're a fool.

ART Then let me be foolish.

> *And exit* ART. ANNE *watches him. And music and fade.*